MOTORMANiA

MOTORBIKES

Written by

PENNY WORMS

First published in 2010 by
Franklin Watts
338 Euston Road
London NW1 3BH

Franklin Watts Australia
Level 17/207 Kent Street
Sydney NSW 2000

Series editor: Jeremy Smith
Design: Graham Rich
Cover design: Graham Rich
Picture research: Penny Worms

A CIP catalogue record for this book is available
from the British Library.

ISBN 978 0 7496 9488 3

Dewey classification: 629.2'275

Printed in China

Franklin Watts is a division of Hachette Children's Books,
an Hachette UK company.
www.hachette.co.uk

The author would like to thank Craig Smith, Felix Wills
and the following for their kind help and permission to
use images: Jerry Hatfield for information about Rollie
Free, Simon Belton at Yamaha Motor (UK) Ltd, Ross
Walker at KTM, and the media team at Honda.

Picture Credits
AMA Motorcycle Hall of Fame: 8. Bike Photo Library:
front cover, 10t, 14, 18cl, 19, 29. Car Culture/Corbis:
9t. Steve Etherington/PAI: 4, 11. Andreas Gradin/
Shutterstock: 24cl. David J Griffin/Corbis: 26bl. Honda:
3, 12, 13t, 13b, 15c, 20, 21l, 21br. Phillip W. Hubbard/
Shutterstock: 27. Hulton Archive/Getty Images: 6 inset t.
KTM-Sportmotorcycle AG: 22bl, 22cr, 23. Clive Mason/
Getty Images: 10b. Leo Mason/Corbis: 26cr. Hughette
Roe/Shutterstock: 19cr. Shutterstock: 5. Peter Stackpole/
Time Life Pictures/Getty Images: 9b. Marjan Veljanoski/
Shutterstock: 6-7 b/g. Yamaha Motor (UK) Ltd: 16,
17c, 17b, 24br, 24-25, 28. Andrew Yates/Getty Images:
15b. Yury Zozlov/Shutterstock: 6 inset b.

Every attempt has been made to clear copyright.
Should there be any inadvertent omission,
please apply to the publisher for rectification.

Disclaimer: Some of the 'Stats and Facts' are
approximations. Others are correct at time of writing,
but will probably change.

CONTENTS

MOTORBIKES 6

VINCENT BLACK SHADOW 8

DUCATI 916 10

HONDA FIREBLADE 12

HONDA VFR750R 14

YAMAHA YZR-M1 16

HARLEY DAVIDSON FATBOY 18

HONDA GOLDWING 20

KTM 690 ENDURO R 22

YAMAHA YZ450F 24

TOP FUEL DRAGBIKE 26

GLOSSARY 28

INDEX 30

MOTORBIKES

Motorbikes are two-wheeled machines. They are cheaper than cars and an easier way to get around. But for those who love motorbikes, it is not just about gliding through traffic. It's about freedom and the sheer thrill of riding.

WARTIME

Motorbikes really began to develop during World War II (1939–45). They were useful to armies (left) because they could travel over difficult ground at speed. After the war, ex-soldiers started to buy motorbikes. They knew that motorbikes weren't just useful, they were also fun!

FEEL THE POWER

The engine is a motorbike's heart. It pumps out enough power to make the motorbike go, but each type of bike needs a different type of engine. All the bikes in this book burn fuel to provide the energy, but how the engines do this makes all the difference in their **performance**.

TYPES OF BIKE

Since the war, different types of motorbike have emerged. Road bikes range from small and nippy to powerful and speedy. There are light, bouncy off-road bikes and super-powerful racing bikes. There are also cruising bikes, designed for comfort on long journeys.

VINCENT BLACK SHADOW

The Vincent Black Shadow is a motorbike legend. It was launched in 1948 and immediately stood out from other **post-war** bikes because of its looks and its astonishing speed. It could cruise along at 161 km/h (100 mph) – faster than any other bike at the time.

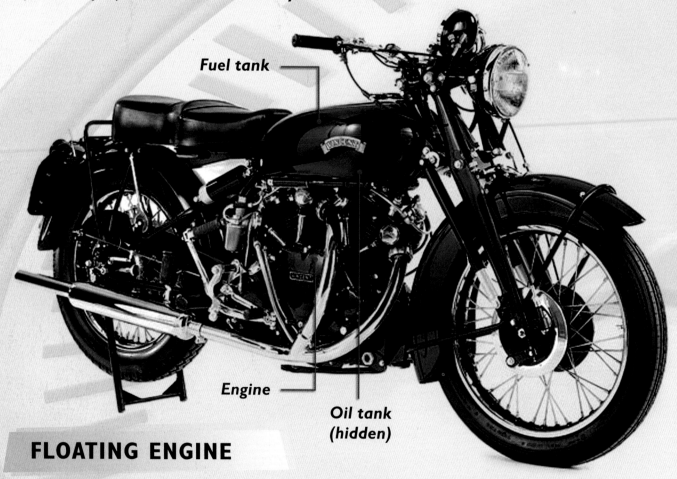

Fuel tank

Engine

Oil tank
(hidden)

FLOATING ENGINE

The Vincent Company came up with a new design. Instead of fixing the engine into the bike's frame, Vincent decided to bolt it on to the oil tank, which was then covered by a big fuel tank. This made it look as if nothing was holding the engine on to the bike.

STATS AND FACTS

- **Top speed:** 198 km/h (123 mph)
- **Engine size:** 998 cc
- **Country of origin:** UK
- **Cost:** £425 in the 1950s, over £10,000 today
- **Claim to fame:** A motorbike classic, which is now highly collectable.

PAINT IT BLACK

The Black Shadow stood out because the bike, its engine and its gearbox were all painted black. It also had a saucer-sized **speedometer** (left) on top of the handlebars.

THE BATHING SUIT BIKE

The Black Shadow was the fastest **production bike** of the time. However, it was its sister bike, the Vincent Black Lightning, that was used to break the Land Speed Record in 1948. The Lightning hit 241.905 km/h (150.313 mph), beating a record set minutes before when the rider, Rollie Free, had his clothes on!

Lying down on the bike with no clothes on helped Rollie Free to gain more speed.

DUCATI 916

In 1994, the motorbike world was stunned when Ducati unveiled the 916 sports bike. Sports bikes are high-performance road bikes, but the 916 was so good it won three World Championships in a row. It was also beautiful and changed the way sports bikes looked forever.

ENGINE POWER

Ducati decided to use a different kind of engine. They called it an 'L-twin', which produced power in smooth, controllable pulses rather than in powerful bursts, like other sports bikes. This gave Ducati racers an advantage. They could begin to **accelerate** out of a bend before anyone else.

DARING DESIGN

The design of the 916 wasn't just about good looks. Ducati had put the **exhaust pipes** under the seat and had added a **fairing** to encase the headlights. This made the bike more **streamlined**.

STATS AND FACTS

- **Top speed:** 254 km/h (158 mph)
- **Engine size:** 916 cc
- **Country of origin:** Italy
- **Cost:** £13,000
- **Claim to fame:** It has earned its place in motorbike history as one of the best bikes of all time.

ROUND THE BEND

When motorbike riders go into a bend at speed, they must brake and lean to one side to get the bike round quickly and smoothly. Only a thin strip of each tyre is in contact with the ground. A burst of power at this point could make the bike slide out of control.

HONDA FIREBLADE

The Honda Fireblade is a sports bike that has set hearts racing since its launch in 1992. The designers and engineers at Honda worked together to produce a lightweight bike with a superbike's engine and excellent handling. The CBR1000RR is the latest Fireblade model.

FIREBLADE EVOLUTION

With the CBR1000RR, the styling is the same as the original Fireblade, but it is lighter, more powerful and with even better balance. It also has many new electronic features.

2010 Fireblade

- **Top speed:** 288 km/h (179 mph)
- **Engine size:** 998 cc
- **Country of origin:** Japan
- **Cost:** £9,221
- **Claim to fame:** The Fireblade is a legendary sports bike and continues to thrill.

1993 Fireblade

EASY RIDING

The Fireblade was an instant success. Riders were impressed by how light, agile and easy to ride it was for such a powerful bike. Honda couldn't produce the bikes fast enough for those who wanted to buy one.

cylinders

IN-LINE FOUR ENGINE

The CBR1000RR has a 998cc 'in-line four engine'. An 'in-line four' has four **cylinders** mounted in a line or row. Inside these cylinders, little explosions take place when a mix of air and fuel is ignited. These explosions generate the power to move the bike's wheels.

HONDA VFR750R

The Honda VFR750R, better known as the RC30, is a bike that was built to win the first-ever World Superbike Championship in 1988. Honda used the most advanced technology of the time so most of the bikes were snapped up by racers. It was rare to see one on the roads.

AERODYNAMICS

If you stick your hand flat out in a strong wind, you can feel the wind pushing it back. If you curl your hand into a fist, the air rushes past your hand, so you don't feel the same push. This is the principle behind the smooth, rounded fairings on the front of the bike. The bike and its rider slice through the air more easily.

STATS AND FACTS

- **Top speed:** 249 km/h (155 mph)
- **Engine size:** 748 cc
- **Country of origin:** Japan
- **Cost:** £8,499
- **Claim to fame:** The first bike to win the World Superbike Championship (see below).

TOP TECHNOLOGY

The RC30 was hand-built by Honda in Japan. They used new materials such as **fibreglass** for the fairings and **titanium** in the engine. The bike also had a single-sided **swing arm** holding the back wheel to the bike. This meant that tyres could be changed easily.

From this side, wheel changes are easy.

SUPERBIKE CHAMPIONSHIP

The bikes racing in the World Superbike Championship are like the bikes available to anyone but they are adapted for the track. This is unlike MotoGP, the other form of motorbike racing. Bike makers build special bikes for MotoGP races (p16).

YAMAHA YZR-M1

Yamaha built the YZR-M1 to race in the MotoGP series of races. No one can buy it, but everyone can admire it, powering around the track driven by motor-racing legend, Valentino Rossi. Rossi helped to develop the bike and has called it 'the greatest bike he has ever ridden'.

MOTOGP

MotoGP is the Formula One of motor racing. Rossi and his Yamaha YZR-M1 compete with the GP bikes of Honda, Kawasaki, Suzuki and Ducati to win the series. Italian car makers, Fiat, are Yamaha's main **sponsor**.

STATS AND FACTS

- **Top speed:** over 320 km/h (199 mph)
- **Engine size:** 800 cc
- **Country of origin:** Japan
- **Cost:** not available to buy
- **Claim to fame:** The best bike in the fastest race series in the world.

PEAK PERFORMANCE

The YZR-M1 is one of the fastest and most advanced racing bikes in the world. It is the result of years of research. The Yamaha racing team are always looking for ways to improve the bike's performance. The lessons they learn on the track are used to improve their road bikes.

TYRE CHOICES

Choosing the right tyres is vital. Very soft, smooth tyres (called slick tyres) are used because the rubber heats up and becomes sticky. This helps the tyres to grip the ground. If it rains, 'wet' tyres with little grooves are needed.

HARLEY DAVIDSON FATBOY

Harley Davidson is an American bike maker, famous for its cruising bikes. The riding positions are upright, so riders can sit back, turn the **throttle** and zoom off to wherever the road takes them. The Fatboy is just one in the range.

THE FATBOY

Wider than most two-wheeled vehicles, the Fatboy deserves its name. However, its looks are classic Harley with lots of shiny **chrome** parts, all beautifully made and on display.

STATS AND FACTS

- **Top speed:** 180 km/h (112 mph)
- **Engine size:** 1584 cc
- **Country of origin:** USA
- **Cost:** £14,530
- **Claim to fame:** Arnold Schwarzenegger rides a Fatboy in the 1994 film, *Terminator*.

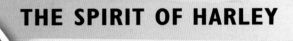

THE SPIRIT OF HARLEY

People talk about the spirit of Harley Davidson just as much as they talk about the bikes. They have been making bikes for over 100 years but in the 1950s and 60s they became the bikes of choice for free riders and bad boys – rebels who took to the open road for the joy of riding.

THE SOUND OF HARLEY

All Harley engines have a distinctive sound. It is a low rumbling sound, as if they are blowing a raspberry to the world as they head off into the sunset.

HONDA GOLDWING

The Goldwing is the best-known touring bike, probably because it has been around for 30 years. Touring bikes are the most comfortable way to travel on two wheels. They are like motorized armchairs with in-built stereos and storage cupboards.

STEADY AS A ROCK

A Goldwing is double the weight of the Honda Fireblade (p12-13). But despite this extra weight, the Goldwing is very stable on the move because its weight is evenly balanced.

STATS AND FACTS

- **Top speed:** 193 km/h (120 mph)
- **Engine size:** 1832 cc
- **Country of origin:** Japan
- **Cost:** £21,451
- **Claim to fame:** The ultimate long-distance tourer and the first motorbike to have an air bag!

COMFORT CRUISING

Touring bikes are designed for long-distance journeys so they need large fuel tanks. The Goldwing can store 25 litres (6.6 gallons) and can go over 320 km (200 miles) without a fill-up. Goldwings also have **cruise control, satellite navigation**, heated seats and hot air blowers to keep the rider's feet warm.

SAFETY FIRST

The most unusual feature on the Goldwing is the air bag system. Like on a car, the air bags inflate to protect the rider in a crash.

KTM 690 ENDURO R

The KTM 690 Enduro R is an off-road bike that can be ridden on the road. Off-road bikes are for those who value freedom over speed or comfort. Instead of traffic lights and cars, they have to contend with rocks, hills and trees – and the 690 Enduro R is an expert.

KTM STYLE

KTM is an Austrian bike maker which specializes in off-road machines. All their bikes are orange and black, but they have added touches of white on the 690 Enduro R to set it apart.

GEARS

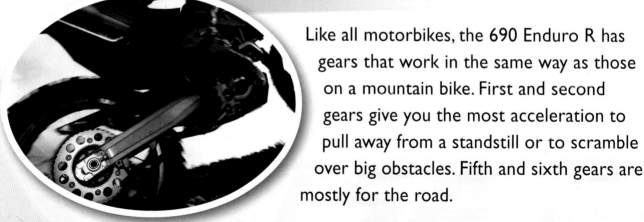

Like all motorbikes, the 690 Enduro R has gears that work in the same way as those on a mountain bike. First and second gears give you the most acceleration to pull away from a standstill or to scramble over big obstacles. Fifth and sixth gears are mostly for the road.

STATS AND FACTS

- **Top speed:** 161 km/h (100 mph)
- **Engine size:** 654 cc
- **Country of origin:** Austria
- **Cost:** £7,195
- **Claim to fame:** An exciting off-roader that is comfortable on the road, too.

OFF-ROAD SPECIALIST

Off-road bikes look different from road bikes. They have small engines, long **suspension systems** and thin tyres. The suspension is a system of springs and **shock absorbers** that work between the wheels and the rider's seat. Without it, the rider would feel every bump and dip in the ground.

YAMAHA YZ450F

The Yamaha YZ450F is an off-road or dirt bike used for **motocross** competitions. It cannot be legally ridden on the roads so it has no lights or number plate. It can, however, tear across dirt tracks, slide around bends and fly through the air over jumps.

MOTOCROSS CHAMPIONS

Motocross is cross-country racing on specially built tracks and trails. It is popular worldwide and bike makers compete to produce race-winning bikes. Yamaha has had more success in the last ten years than any other bike maker.

CHAIN DRIVEN

Just like a mountain bike, a chain drives the wheels of the Yamaha YZ450F, but the engine provides the power, not the rider's legs. The engines are small but produce enough power to accelerate sharply and keep high speeds on the straights.

STATS AND FACTS

- **Top speed:** 161 km/h (100 mph)
- **Engine size:** 450 cc
- **Country of origin:** Japan
- **Cost:** £7,100
- **Claim to fame:** The 2009 World Championship winning bike.

BUMPS AND JUMPS

Motocross tracks have steep climbs, drop downs, jumps, fast straights and sharp corners. Dirt bikes need to be light, agile, stable and powerful. Their suspensions need to be strong. Their tyres need good grip. And the riders? They need to be fit and fearless!

TOP FUEL DRAGBIKE

A dragbike is a heavily adapted racing bike. There are many categories of dragbike, from street bikes to the fastest top-fuel machines (which burn rocket fuel). However, the races are the same. Two machines line up side-by-side on a drag strip. When the lights go on, the riders unleash the bikes' awesome power in a race to the finish.

BURNOUT!

The tyres are heated up at the start by letting them spin when the bike is standing still to make the rubber more sticky. This is called a 'burnout' because when water is sprayed on them, it causes a lot of steam! The tyres need replacing after only eight runs.

WHEELIE BAR

Most dragbikes have a long metal frame bolted to the back of the bike with little wheels on the end. This stops the bike from flipping over backwards at the start of the race when all that power could cause the front wheel to take off like a plane.

- **Top speed:** 384 km/h (239 mph)
- **Engine size:** no maximum
- **Country of origin:** often Japan
- **Cost:** over £50,000 to build
- **Claim to fame:** Dragbikes are the fastest bikes in the world!

SPIDERMAN

Larry 'Spiderman' McBride is a top-fuel racing champion and world record holder for the fastest dragbike run. His bike went down the 402 metre ($\frac{1}{4}$ mile) strip in 5.74 seconds, reaching 100 km/h (62 mph) in under one second!

GLOSSARY

accelerate to pick up speed

chrome a shiny, silvery metal

cruise control a device that, when switched on, maintains the speed of a vehicle, so the rider doesn't need to use the throttle (accelerator)

cylinders tube-like chambers in which a mix of petrol and air is burned to power a vehicle

exhaust pipes pipes that carry waste gases away from the engine and releases them into the air

fairing the rounded front on some bikes that is fitted to make the bike cut through the air easily

fibreglass a hard, flexible material made from tiny fibres of glass

motocross a series of cross-country motorbike races

peformance the way a vehicle performs or behaves

post-war after World War II

production bike bikes that are made in a factory and go on sale to anyone

satellite navigation a device that uses information from satellites in space to tell drivers where they are and which way to go

shock absorbers air or oil-filled devices that soak up bumps in the road

speedometer a device on a vehicle that shows at what speed it is going

sponsor a company that gives money for something, often to advertise themselves or their products

streamlined shaped to allow air or water to flow over or around it

suspension systems a system of springs and shock absorbers that work between the body of a vehicle and its wheels

swing arm a metal arm that holds the back wheel in place

throttle the part on the handlebars of a bike that, when twisted, releases fuel into the engine to make the bike go faster (also known as an accelerator)

titanium a strong metal that resists rust

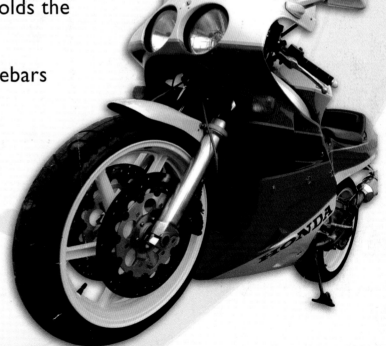

INDEX

A

aerodynamics 14

C

cruising bikes 7, 18-19

D

dirt bikes 24-25
dragbikes 26-27
Ducati 916 10-11

F

Free, Rollie 9

H

Harley Davidson Fatboy 18-19
Honda Fireblade 12-13, 20
Honda Goldwing 20-21
Honda VFR750R 14-15

K

KTM 690 Enduro R 22-23

M

McBride, Larry 'Spiderman' 27
motocross 24-25, 28
MotoGP races 15, 16-17

O

off-road bikes 7, 22-23, 24-25

R

racing bikes 7, 14-15, 16-17, 26-27
road bikes 7, 10-11, 17
Rossi, Valentino 16

S

speedometer 9, 29
sports bikes 10-11, 12-13
suspension 23, 25, 29

T

touring bikes 20-21
tyres 11, 17, 23, 25, 26

V

Vincent Black Lightning 9
Vincent Black Shadow 8-9

W

World Superbike Championships 14, 15
World War II 6

Y

Yamaha YZR-M1 16-17
Yamaha YZ450F 24-25